No School Today

A Book about Nouns

by Cari Meister
illustrated by Holli Conger

amicus readers 3

Say Hello to Amicus Readers.

You'll find our helpful dog, Amicus, chasing a ball—to let you know the reading level of a book.

1

Learn to Read

High frequency words and close photo-text matches introduce familiar topics and provide support for brand new readers.

2

Read Independently

Some repetition is mixed with varied sentence structures and a select amount of new vocabulary words are introduced with text and photo support.

3

Read to Know More

Interesting facts and engaging art and photos give fluent readers fun books both for reading practice and to learn about new topics.

Amicus Readers are published by Amicus
P.O. Box 1329, Mankato, MN 56002
www.amicuspublishing.us

Illustrations by Holli Conger
Editor Wendy Dieker
Designer Heather Dreisbach

Printed in the United States of America.

10 9 8 7 6 5 4 3 2 1

Library of Congress Cataloging-in-Publication Data
Names: Meister, Cari, author. | Conger, Holli, illustrator.
Title: No school today : a book about nouns / by Cari Meister ; illustrated by Holli Conger.
Description: Mankato, Minnesota : Amicus, [2016] | Series: Say what? Parts of Speech | Audience: K to Grade 3._
Identifiers: LCCN 2015042132 (print) | LCCN 2015046376 (ebook) | ISBN 9781607539346 (library binding) | ISBN 9781681510583 (eBook)
Subjects: LCSH: English language--Noun--Juvenile literature.
Classification: LCC PE1201 .M45 2016 (print) | LCC PE1201 (ebook) | DDC 428.2--dc23
LC record available at http://lccn.loc.gov/2015042132

A noun is a **person**, **place**, or **thing**. The **purple** words in the story are nouns.

Scarlett peeks out the **window**. "Hooray!" she shouts.

The reporter on TV says, "Snow is falling all over Wisconsin. All schools in Benton are closed."

Scarlett puts on boots, a scarf, mittens, and a coat.

BENTON SCHOOLS CLOSED TODAY
2

Arjun and Ping are already outside.

"Hi, Scarlett," says Arjun. "We are making a ramp of snow. Do you want to help?"

"Sure!" Scarlett goes to the garage and gets a shovel and sled.

The friends scoop snow.
The friends pack snow.
The ramp is done.

Ping puts her scarf on a stick.

"Let's see if we can slide down the hill past the stick," she says.

Arjun goes to the top.

"Here I go!" he says.

Arjun slides and jumps. He glides to the tree.

Scarlett goes next.

"WHEEE!" she screams as she jumps. Scarlett glides to the rock.

Ping goes last.

"Here I come!" she says.

"Whoa!" Ping says as she flies through the air. Her sled glides. She zooms past the stick. Ping wins!

Jobs of a Noun

A noun can be a person:
"Hi, Scarlett," says Arjun.

It can be a place:
All schools in Benton are closed.

It can be a thing:
The ramp is done.

A noun can be a proper name, which needs a capital letter:
Snow is falling all over Wisconsin.

It can be a common noun with a lowercase letter:
The snowstorm covered the whole state.